#WILAY
What I Love About You

Stormy Weathers

For my favorite
yoga instructor,
Vicki !
Love,
Toni
aka Stormy

#WILAY

What I Love About You

By Stormy Weathers

He is mine.

Dedicated to the Love of My Life

P.J.W.

As I begin to write, my hazel eyes riveted to the screen and fingers positioned on the keyboard, I glance down at the letters u and I—u always with i. U always before I. How apposite is that? Coincidences are not credible, but I am a believer in Godcidences. You are a Godcidence. So, maybe my inspiration for this book was divine.

When we began dating, I carried my phone turned up in my palm like a heart transplant patient eagerly waiting for news about a donor—always waiting on a text from you.

Now I want to tell you everything I love about you, yet words seem inadequate. Sometimes people don't know what they have until it's gone. Yet, that's not the case with us. In truth, I feel fortunate beyond all deserving to be with you and bereft at the prospect of ever losing you.

And I'm not alone. Others see the fantastic things that make you so loveable.

So, where do I begin to tell our story of a love that has no end?

Dear Readers,

The year is 2023. By now, viral, outbreak, and pandemic are the last words most of you want to read. Simply reading the words can conjure up negative emotions. There is a reason we can easily recall adverse events and feelings. Negative emotions scream at you and stick, while positive ones only whisper and then quickly slide away. In other words, positive memories and words are like Teflon—almost nothing sticks, and negative ones are like Velcro. This fact is the basis for the magic five-to-one ratio. For every negative interaction between partners, there must be five positive ones. Stable and happy couples share many more positive messages than negative ones.

In #WILAY, I share a simple two-minute phenomenon. This miracle is based on the fact that one of the most effective ways of feeling inner peace and finding happiness is by being grateful. #WILAY is a collection of intimate and romantic messages women can replicate with creative, personalized touches and emojis to express gratitude to a loved one in daily texts or love notes. It works because you will continue to think about the positive attribute or thing you wrote even after you send the message. Your gratitude and appreciation will grow and blossom day by day. After all, appreciation and gratitude never grow old. No one can ever have too much appreciation or gratitude, yet we tend to neglect this as time passes in a relationship. Giving praise and showing appreciation for every single thing, no matter how minuscule it may seem, will make a world of difference to the quality of your relationships and your well-being.

I intentionally minimized graphics to encourage readers to select their pictures and emojis. Highlight or tab entries that resonate with you and make them your own. Use the final pages to record private notes. Then, begin expressing your love in daily messages. Remember to include #WILAY so that WILAY goes wild and viral! Spread positive influence, not influenza!

Chapter One

Only the Beginning

#WILAY 01 January: January is a time of new beginnings. Like the meaning of the rare and unique name, Jenara, you are joyful, encouraging, and passionate.

#WILAY 02 January: I love how you find happiness in everyday miracles like sunrises, sunsets, and the moon.

#WILAY 03 January: You help me with difficult decisions where there is no ideal answer.

#WILAY 04 January: I love how you kiss me on the forehead and whisper words like "Take it easy." When you do that, I am ok. I'm not afraid anymore.

#WILAY 05 January: I love the names you give to wild animals like the rabbits, "Sidewalk" and "Track." And you even named the critters that inch their way up into our backyard, Muskrat Susie and Muskrat Sam.

#WILAY 6 January: You help me in times of sorrow and grief. Your presence makes painful experiences a little less difficult.

#WILAY 07 January: I love your patience. I don't think you've ever told me to hurry. On the contrary, you quietly sit back and wait. Patience is one of the hundreds of things I love about you.

#WILAY 08 January: I love how we enjoy long walks on the beach, then sit silently on a weathered wooden bench to enjoy a splendid seacoast sunset and a wintry breeze.

#WILAY 09 January: You showed me that sharing a life with someone who loves me just the way I am is possible.

#WILAY 10 January: I admire your musical talent. I'm so proud when I watch your performances from my seat in the audience.

#WILAY 11 January: You're a very generous tipper. And I kind of love that about you—sort of.

#WILAY 12 January: I love how you hold me and tell me not to be scared.

#WILAY 13 January: I love your hair—the way it sweeps off your forehead. You are very handsome.

#WILAY 14 January: You pick up the slack when I need you to. I love that you appreciate a clean and orderly home (almost as much as I do).

#WILAY 15 January: You taught me that acceptance is the nature of true friendship and love, not judgment. To be entirely accepted by another, for better or for worse, is to feel safe at home, finally.

#WILAY 16 January: I love how we share insights and reflections, like this well-known aphorism: *Think before you speak.*

Is it **T**rue?
Is it **H**elpful?
Is it **I**mportant or **I**nspiring?
Is it **N**ecessary?
Is it **K**ind?

*Let your words heal,
not wound.*

#WILAY 17 January: I love that we share moonrises. The first full moon of 2022 rose on 17 January. It was called the full Wolf Moon. I'd name our moon Aruna. This name of Japanese origin means "moon love." I love you to the moon and back.

#WILAY 18 January: You are a good listener and give others a chance to be heard.

#WILAY 19 January: Observation is your superpower. You are a skillful photographer and graphic designer. You recognize the beauty in everyday life and notice things others may ignore.

#WILAY 20 January: I love how you bend down slightly to kiss my forehead as you gently hug me. I think you do this instinctively. I was at peace when you held me yesterday. My heart recognized you as part of its own.

#WILAY 21 January: You never stop trying to grow and evolve as a person. And you take me along—constantly introducing me to new things and pieces of life I might have missed otherwise.

#WILAY 22 January: You value time more than money and possessions. It reminds me of a Tolstoy quote I like: "There is no past and no future; no one has ever entered those two imaginary kingdoms. There is only the present." The present time, my love. I want to be present with you.

#WILAY 23 January: I love that you're from Massachusetts with your very sexy Boston accent and childhood memories of ice skating on frozen lakes, playing hockey, trips to Dunkin', and family vacations to the Cape.

#WILAY 24 January: I love how we select television series, like *Six Feet Under* and so many others. We look forward to watching films and documentaries together.

#WILAY 25 January: You always give your honest opinion even when you know I won't like it.

#WILAY 26 January: I love your preferences in music (like Chicago) and your keen ability to discern quality. You appreciate diverse genres from classical pieces to the improvisation of jazz. That's special.

#WILAY 27 January: I love the sound of your voice, especially in the morning when it is deep and gruff—low in pitch and sexy.

#WILAY 28 January: You can watch reruns of legendary sitcoms like *M*A*S*H* and never get bored with the shows. I love simple things like that.

#WILAY 29 January: I love how you capture scenic landscapes and tap into your creativity by photoshopping pictures to perfection—even ones of us. You always make me feel prettier than I am.

#WILAY 30 January: I love how we can sit for a while, saying nothing, a couple comfortable in a long silence—simply being together with no phones, no idle chit-chat—just presence.

Image by Gordon Johnson from Pixabay

#WILAY 31 January: I love your spontaneity and willingness to try exciting new things like thrilling roller coasters. We're an adventuresome duo.

Chapter Two

February

#WILAY 01 February: Valen is a name meaning strong and healthy, adjectives that also describe you.

#WILAY 02 February: You encourage me not to suffer imagined troubles. I appreciate that because worry is only a waste of time.

#WILAY 03 February: You understand the difference between healthy vs. not healthy in a holistic way—spiritually, mentally, physically, socially, and cognitively.

#WILAY 04 February: I love that you understand the difference between helpful and not helpful.

#WILAY 05 February: You enjoy fine dining at "hole in the wall" regional restaurants where the food is always delicious, but your company is even better.

#WILAY 06 February: When you hug me, I understand that you are my home. I feel so loved, secure, and peaceful in your arms.

#WILAY 07 February: I appreciate that I don't have to think too hard or too long to come up with something else I love about you every day. Today? I love that you always immediately buy things when we need them, like a household supply or even a dog bowl. I never need to ask more than once.

#WILAY 08 February: I appreciate it when you give your full attention to me. I admire that ability (which I often lack). Attention is a limited resource. We only have so much to offer. Thanks for spending yours on me.

#WILAY 09 February: You have an aura of tranquility. On the other hand, I'm impatient and often intolerant. Sometimes, I am even out of control and hard to handle, but you can always reel me in.

#WILAY 10 February: I love how you always try to make relationships work.

#WILAY 11 February: You give me the kind of feelings that people write poetry about.

#WILAY 12 February: You try hard to settle us when we disagree with the slightest, most gentle touch—a tactile agreement.

#WILAY 13 February: You patiently teach me about football and hockey even when I ask the same questions game after game—time and time again. 🏈

#WILAY Valentine's Day: You alone can touch my heart and soul. It's your love that has so often calmed my doubts and fears. It's your love that gives me inspiration.

#WILAY 15 February: You exude kindness to others and always with a gentle, innocent smile.

 #WILAY 16 February: You are our financier; you make a habit of studying finances, economic trends, and investing. We need your expertise in this area, because I'm only a coupon clipper and discount shopper.

#WILAY 17 February: Your love is irreplaceable. You bought a necklace for me with two interlocking rings and said it reminded you of our love. For me, it symbolizes love as a circle with no beginnings and no endings.

#WILAY 18 February: You introduce me to new technology like the latest iPhone to replace a Blackberry (some younger readers may not understand, but a Blackberry is not a fruit). Then you started sending lovely text messages that would brighten up my days.

#WILAY 19 February: You always turn the dial to my favorite radio stations.

#WILAY 20 February: You participate in our couple's sessions with a desire that we both learn and grow. You show empathy when I share fears, making me feel that you deeply understand. We are growing, and our goals are aligned.

#WILAY 21 February: You are capable of a deep-souled relationship as much as the basic forms of care, like being sure I don't forget to brush my teeth at bedtime!

#WILAY 22 February: Despite the fear and uncertainty, you still love me. I love you, too. I'm here and willing to see all of it through as long as you're by my side.

#WILAY 23 February: I love the thoughtfulness you put into Valentine's Day cards. I read them over and over and over.

#WILAY 24 February: I love the sound of your heartbeat when I rest my head on your chest. My heart synchronizes with yours, and we become one—we are whole.

#WILAY 25 February: I love the rare but precious times where spontaneity wins over careful planning, like waking up and deciding to go for a beach walk—those unplanned experiences that lack the build-up of expectations.

#WILAY 26 February: You can easily go with the flow: unselfish, curious, patient.

#WILAY 27 February: You're always willing to let me send items from my wish list to your email, and soon a gift magically appears on our front doorstep.

#WILAY 28 February: I love that you, like me, find joy in nature like a specially crafted bluebird feeder outside the kitchen window that brings joy year after year.

Chapter Three

March

#WILAY 01 March: I love how John Varvatos Vintage cologne mixes with your body's chemistry to create an irresistible, masculine scent.

#WILAY 02 March: I love your terms of endearment for Winter (the dog), like "Hi, handsome." We're both wagging our tails when you walk through the door. I know he's happy when you are home. I am, too.

#WILAY 03 March: I love that you're still here.

#WILAY 04 March: I love your positivity. Nobody knows how to put a positive spin on things as well as you do. I can serve you a partially cooked meal, yet you're grateful to be trying a new dish. You always seek out the good.

#WILAY 05 March: You have emotional intelligence. You know that the most profound work is done in partnership (union) with two heart-connected individuals seeing the issues that trigger each other as a gift, or a clue, to their healing rather than an obstacle.

#WILAY 06 March: I love that you are trying, even though it's hard work when I display reassurance-seeking behaviors like rapidly firing questions to reduce my uncertainty.

#WILAY 07 March: On a rainy, windy Sunday morning, you take me out for a wholesome early breakfast with the promise of an afternoon nap. You fill my belly and fulfill my heart.

#WILAY 08 March: You encourage me to be fully in the moment— to be all there, wherever we are.

#WILAY 09 March: You are handsome and sexy.

#WILAY 10 March: You invest in yourself, especially in learning new things and caring for your body and mind.

#WILAY 11 March: You remind me to also take care of myself, like drinking more water, consuming less alcohol, and avoiding caffeine later in the day. That makes me feel like you are just as vested in my well-being as in your own.

#WILAY 12 March: You love Winter, our four-legged child.

#WILAY 13 March: You don't hesitate to hush me down and remind me to be "softer" and more subtle. You polish me and smooth my rough edges.

#WILAY 14 March: You have such a wonderful, innocent smile, but you've been practicing for a long time. Here's the proof.

#WILAY 15 March: You always seem to appreciate my cooking. All we need is love and a good meal, but a little 😉 dessert now and then doesn't hurt either—if you know what I mean.

#WILAY 16 March: You support me and want me to be successful. You celebrate my accomplishments.

#WILAY 17 March: You put thought into surprises like making Irish coffee on Saint Patrick's Day.

#WILAY 18 March: You take time to find answers to questions, such as when I asked about the name of a March full moon.

#WILAY 19 March: You willingly take risks and travel with me toward positive changes for better mental, physical, social, and spiritual health.

#WILAY 20 March: I love that you are teaching me that when I have pains, I don't need to be one.

#WILAY 21 March: You are a self-professed introvert. Thanks for telling me I should not take it personally when you are "introverting." We're opposites, but extroverts need introverts in their lives and vice-versa. Our differences perfectly complement each other.

#WILAY 22 March: Yes, the vows say 'in sickness and in health' and 'for better or worse,' but that's like clicking "I agree" to the terms and conditions when you download an app or program on the internet. You don't think any of the bad will ever pertain to you. I love you because you are still here for better and worse. And the better will come. I promise.

#WILAY 23 March: I love your 'Paulisms,' Words of Wisdom from Paul. You said, "Discussion is always better than argument because an argument is to find WHO is right, and discussion is to find WHAT is right." And that is right.

#WILAY 24 March: I love you because you are worthy of my trust, and I can hand over financial matters to you without reluctance or worry.

#WILAY 25 March: I love how you sometimes greet me with a warm embrace and kiss on my forehead when I least expect it.

#WILAY 26 March: You helped me understand that self-love is not selfish. You can never truly love another until you love yourself.

#WILAY 27 March: You are a sports enthusiast and faithfully champion the Bruins and Patriots.

#WILAY 28 March: I love that you move from the recliner to the couch and massage my aching feet even when you are tired and sleepy.

#WILAY 29 March: I love how you surprise me with thoughtfully selected gifts. You know me.

#WILAY 30 March: I enjoy the times when you come home and "just be." I need to be better at giving you space to relax, unwind, and de-stress.

#WILAY 31 March: Sometimes I am just stopped in my tracks in awe of the considerate things you do, like wiping down the interior of the microwave because you know I like it spick and span.

Chapter Four

April

#WILAY 01 April: It's April Fool's Day, and I am looking out for a prank! I love the way you tease me! I enjoy your jokes and playful antics, like peering into the kitchen window to startle me as I clean dishes (just like you did with your mom). 🙀

#WILAY 02 April: I love that you allow me to stand on your shoulders so I can glimpse farther down the road, far beyond this challenging part of our journey.

#WILAY 03 April: I love how you always put effort, concern, and time into our relationship. Words are a dime a dozen, but actions are worth billions.

#WILAY 04 April: I love the way your naked body feels wrapped snugly around mine.

#WILAY 05 April: You are a better version of yourself every time I see you.

#WILAY 06 April: I love that you have high morals of conduct, such as when you didn't take advantage of my promiscuous behavior after I indulged in too much wine. Later, when you finally did lay beside me, your words were, "Isn't it so much better when we are both here?" The answer was and still is yes. So much better.

#WILAY 07 April: Like me, I love that you want to be more fulfilled in some areas of your life. How we treat one another, our behaviors will determine if we find fulfillment together or alone. I cannot push you away and expect you to still be there when I change my mind. So, I'm sorry if it sometimes feels like I'm pulling you back. I don't want the most incredible catch of my life, my Pisces, to swim away.

#WILAY 08 April: I love the way you are easygoing, patient, and unhurried.

#WILAY: 09 April: I love the way your introversion forms its own kind of companionship—you (Me) and your two best friends (Myself and I).

#WILAY 10 April: You keep me optimistic. You're not only my last hope. You are my highest hope for a brighter future.

#WILAY 11 April: I love the lub-dub of your heartbeat and the pace of your breathing, connecting so profoundly that your biorhythms are in perfect synch with mine.

#WILAY 12 April: You are doing everything to keep us together against people and forces wedging us apart.

#WILAY 13 April: I love that you willingly wear pink. The color pink is also thought to be a calming color associated with love and kindness. Even when decked out as the Easter Bunny, it suits you well.

#WILAY 14 April: I love that you once said we were planting seeds that would grow into a magnificent oak. Oak trees grow stronger in contrary winds. We are sturdy. Together we will endure the storm.

#WILAY 15 April: You never "tax" me.

#WILAY 16 April: You are comfortable enough to be silent. Silence is sometimes our friend. The problem is that I sometimes struggle with the urge to fill it.

#WILAY 17 April: My Darling, I love the many ways you show affection. I feel blessed this Easter morning, not only to have found my soulmate but for that soulmate to be you. Miracles do happen.

#WILAY 18 April: I love how you value time and close relationships more than anything else.

#WILAY 19 April: You broaden my horizons in so many ways. For example, I love that you suggest delectable and savory dishes I've never eaten, from simple nutrient-dense foods like sweet potatoes and avocados to cuisine from different cultures I might never have tasted.

#WILAY 20 April: I admire the way you are able to let go of the small stuff.

#WILAY 21 April: You desire positive things, such as happiness and health, but do more than wistfully dream for optimal outcomes. Hope is not a strategy. You engage with the path of practice that leads to fulfilling goals.

#WILAY 22 April: You treat me to my favorite strawberry cake with buttercream icing on my birthday.

#WILAY 23 April: (I'm sneaking this one in for our dog, Winter Weathers). I am overjoyed when you take me for long walks and car rides. Woof!

#WILAY 24 April: I find your chest hair incredibly sexy! It is so comforting to rest my head on your chest and feel the prickly warmth of your hair on my cheek.

#WILAY 25 April: I love the way you kiss me. I enjoy being on the receiving end of your impressive kissing repertoire, from affectionate pecks on the forehead to long, sensual kisses as we snuggle on the couch.

#WILAY 26 April: You sometimes patiently stand aside and watch as I enjoy activities like brushing the dog. You never seem to mind my "busyness."

#WILAY 27 April: You show appreciation with tips at a restaurant or as gratuity for a hairdresser. You don't barter and haggle because a few pennies more is not going to break your bank, but it may help the local farmer selling his vegetables at the market. You are making deposits into the karma bank!

#WILAY 28 April: I love how you understand that nothing is more dynamic and effective than a positive thought coupled with positive action. Behavior is very telling.

#WILAY 29 April: You helped me to understand that a positive mindset brings about positive things.

#WILAY April 30: You are strong like a giant redwood whose roots run deep and wide. I love your endurance and strength.

Chapter Five

May

#WILAY 01 May: Darling, this is our month! We celebrate the day we first met and our anniversary. Springtime reminds me that we each show our love and feel loved differently. You express love by sharing quality time in many ways, such as reading a book aloud, scheduling date nights, or just going on a walk together around the block. I'm so fortunate to share time with you.

#WILAY 02 May: You being here (still) makes every day better.

#WILAY 03 May: You help me in many ways, even with menial tasks like laundry.

#WILAY 04 May: I love how you see the world through a positive lens. Yes, it's a cliché, but you look at the world from the bright side.

#WILAY 05 May: I enjoy celebrating Cinco de Mayo with you. Let's fiesta all day, siesta all night, or vice versa!

#WILAY 06 May: You always catch me when I fall. You are my hero, my Superman.

#WILAY 07 May: I appreciate your taking the time to read my text messages, blogs, and books, even when the genre isn't one of your favorites.

#WILAY 08 May: You always find the perfect cards, from the most romantic to the comical! One of my favorites is the Mother's Day card from the dog. A dog on his hind legs pushing a vacuum. I heard the loud humming vibrations of a vacuum cleaner when I opened the card. White noise to my ears!

#WILAY 09 May: I love that you are a personal finance enthusiast and sometimes even join forces with my frugal ways, like saving pennies at the pumps and using coupons. I can pinch a nickel so hard that the buffalo screams!

#WILAY 10 May: I love your discerning taste in home décor. You once said that we should accessorize with photographs and objects that tell our story. Your stylishness makes our space aesthetically pleasing, comfortable, and functional. Thanks for letting me buy an ottoman to prop my feet on at the end of the day!

#WILAY 11 May: You had me the day you helped me decide to go forward with surgery to repair my pet's damaged knee ligament. It added many dog years and quality to his life.

#WILAY 12 May: Sometimes the simplest things mean the most. Thank you for taking the time to help me find my fitness tracker. You gave it to me as a birthday gift, and I was sad when I thought I had lost it forever.

#WILAY 13 May: I love the sound of your laugh and your way of finding joy in little moments.

#WILAY 14 May: I love your abundance mindset. You have generosity of spirit and feel sincerely happy for other people's success. You know there are more than enough resources and love to go around, not just for some, but for everyone.

#WILAY 15 May: I can never get enough of your sexy masculinity.

#WILAY 16 May: You watch television programs and movies that I suggest (even though our preferences differ), and you are not annoyed when my selection turns out to be a letdown.

#WILAY 17 May: You provided me with the will, the drive, and the strength to withdraw from old patterns of self-destruction.

#WILAY 18 May: I love how you kiss me with your full lips and the practiced embouchure of a wind instrumentalist.

#WILAY 19 May: Sometimes the most significant source of stress is in our minds. You sometimes need to tell that negative committee meeting in my head to sit down and shut up! I appreciate how you help me let go of hurtful mindsets like guilt, perfectionism, and regret.

#WILAY 20 May: I love how you embrace me in a heart-to-heart hug when sharing good news.

#WILAY 21 May: You are my accountability partner. You help me keep commitments and show me the detours around roadblocks.

#WILAY 22 May: I love that you play music for the church. I could chalk your skill up to talent, but I know you have practiced a lifetime to become the accomplished musician you are today.

#WILAY 23 May: Your presence improves my life, and I wouldn't want it any other way.

#WILAY 24 May: I love how you never stop trying, no matter how broken we are. If I had to, I would crawl to you on broken limbs because I'm a fighter, too. No matter what happens, I will never regret loving you.

#WILAY 25 May: You can make time feel like it's passing by incredibly quickly. When I'm with you, hours feel like seconds, and when we are apart, days feel like years.

#WILAY 26 May: You are a top gun in everything you do! You can be my wingman anytime! When I ask you to do something, you do it even if you have to figure it out. And I never have to ask more than once.

#WILAY 27 May: An affirmation: I love that you married me. Every day I'm still discovering new things about you to love.

#WILAY 28 May: You add sugar, spice, and flavor to my life as we explore a variety of cuisines from around the globe.

#WILAY 29 May: You always open my car door. Such a gentleman!

#WILAY 30 May: Happy Anniversary of the Day We Met. I love you because everything you are is something I have never come across before, never in this lifetime. When we met, my heart already knew and whispered, "He's the one."

#WILAY 31 May: I'm a better person when I'm with you.

Chapter Six

June

#WILAY 1 June: You give me courage and faith—a serene place between the way things are and the way things are yet to be.

#WILAY 2 June: You were our daughter's first love the night you danced with her in the moonlight at a father-daughter ball.

#WILAY 3 June: Even now, the best in me sees the best in you.

#WILAY 4 June: I've never felt more comfortable around any other person.

#WILAY 5 June: You had me when you said that love isn't only a feeling; it's an art. And like any art, it takes more than inspiration. It's hard work.

#WILAY 6 June: I look at you and smile for no reason.

#WILAY 7 June: You listen so attentively to details of my day that you could be my biographer. I tell you things I would never share with another soul, and you absorb everything I say and want to hear more.

#WILAY 8 June: I cherish your absolute devotion and fidelity.

#WILAY 9 June: I feel treasured when you call me by the endearment, "My Love."

#WILAY 10 June: After we dated for a while, you thoughtfully asked if you should introduce me as your friend or girlfriend. I secretly wished for fiancé and best friend.

#WILAY 11 June: Your love keeps no records of wrongs.

#WILAY 12 June: I love how you attentively listen when I tell a joke, even when it takes me five minutes to reach the punchline. I never feel the necessity to condense my stories.

#WILAY 13 June: You always follow the golden rule.

#WILAY 14 June: You are patriotic. Perhaps that's why Flag Day is your favorite holiday!

#WILAY 15 June: We each warm to the sound of the other's voice.

#WILAY 16 June: You make me feel so young and bring meaning to my life.

#WILAY 17 June: I love your honesty, always dispensed with genuine compassion and in carefully measured doses. You keep me growing in significant ways. I'm grateful you care enough to tell me things I need to hear.

#WILAY 18 June: I love the clothes you wear. Your style exudes masculinity and comfort.

#WILAY 19 June: You are my human shield, my knight in shining armor.

#WILAY 20 June: You usually enjoy whatever I maneuver you into doing—museums, festivals, day trips, even shopping.

#WILAY 21 June: You are very patient with my mishaps (even when I recklessly backed the car into our garage door). You told me not to worry even though the door was totaled.

#WILAY 22 June: I love the perfect size of your body, of how small I feel next to you. It's very calming.

#WILAY 23 June: You placed wind chimes outside our bedroom window, enhancing our space with gentle, melodic sounds, positive energy, and harmony.

#WILAY 24 June: I love how you patiently idled for over an hour in a sultry afternoon traffic jam so we could eat at my favorite restaurant on the other side of a bridge-tunnel.

#WILAY 25 June: Your comical side is one of the things I fell in love with.

#WILAY 26 June: Sometimes you seem just beyond my reach, but unattainability is often attractive.

#WILAY 27 June: You gently brush off my sandy toes after beach walks, and the world shrinks to our bench, your hands, my feet.

#WILAY 28 June: Your love always protects, trusts, and perseveres.

#WILAY 29 June: Instead of being all-consumed by your own needs, you tend to the needs of others.

#WILAY 30 June: You are humble and gracious, showing appreciation by bowing to the audience after a spectacular musical performance.

Chapter Seven

July

#WILAY 1 July: You are a reliable provider. Our material needs are always satisfied (and then some).

#WILAY 2 July: You believe in me.

#WILAY 3 July: You are always there when I need you.

#WILAY 4 July: You make my world sparkle like fireworks on the Fourth of July, a starlit sky, and a diamond mine.

#WILAY 5 July: Your plans and dreams blend with mine, becoming ours. Then, we make our dreams come true.

#WILAY 6 July: You bring me chai lattes and bean crème Frappuccino drinks, even though you think the prices are absurd.

#WILAY 7 July: You are my trusted confidante.

#WILAY 8 July: I appreciate how you tend to the yard. The grass is always greener on our side of the fence, and the lawn is not even artificial. It's the real thing! WE are the real thing!

#WILAY 9 July: You helped me develop sound financial habits.

#WILAY 10 July: You've shown me the importance of compromise in relationships.

#WILAY 11 July: You taught me that every fight is not worth fighting; sometimes, it's better to let things go. Sometimes the battle is within ourselves.

#WILAY 12 July: You stand up to me when I'm wrong, making me stronger and accountable.

#WILAY 13 July: With you, I have unforgettable memories. Every moment with you is fleeting but gives way to cherished and timeless memories.

#WILAY 14 July: You remain faithful in your promises and obligations.

#WILAY 15 July: Even amid trials and tribulations, moments with you make life not only bearable and worth living but filled with hope. Thanks for coming along with me on this journey. Let's not let the potholes get in our way.

#WILAY 16 July: You are my strength when I am weak.

#WILAY 17 July: You know how to have fun.

#WILAY 18 July: You showed me that love is kind, forgiving, and patient.

#WILAY 19 July: You're never more than a text or phone call away. I love it when you call and say that you only want to hear the sound of my voice.

#WILAY 20 July: You always seem eager to hear about my day.

#WILAY 21 July: I love your impeccable integrity. You do the right thing even when no one is looking.

#WILAY 22 July: You love unconditionally.

#WILAY 23 July: You fill my days and nights with love and affection.

#WILAY 24 July: You treat me as an equal.

#WILAY 25 July: You never tire of hugs and kisses.

#WILAY 26 July: You understand and respect my personal space.

#WILAY 27 July: Your arms, heart, and mind are always open. You show love without restraint.

#WILAY 28 July: You are a force of optimism, positivity and kindness in this crazy world.

#WILAY 29 July: You've seen me in the darkness, yet you still appreciate everything about me that shines.

#WILAY 30 July: You have faith in God.

#WILAY 31 July: I love how strong and confidant you are.

Chapter Eight

August

#WILAY 01 August: You make our life together so rich and fulfilling.

#WILAY 02 August: I know you would do anything for me.

#WILAY 03 August: You've made our lives better in so many ways.

#WILAY 04 August: You make our days and nights together worth remembering.

#WILAY 05 August: You are my companion, my guide.

#WILAY 06 August: Your heart is always true. I trust you.

#WILAY 07 August: Your love is the kind that accepts and forgives. It is kind and caring.

#WILAY 08 August: You find the most incredible, latest gadgets.

#WILAY 09 August: I love the way you carefully ponder your words, even when texting. Your texts are few but always kind, cheerful, and considerate.

#WILAY 10 August: Whenever I reach out, you take my hand.

#WILAY 11 August: A man who cooks is attractive, but a man who does the dishes is irresistible. You do both!

#WILAY 12 August: I love how you find happiness watching as I feed seagulls, beginning with one or two who squawk for their family and friends. Before long, we have a beach party.

#WILAY 13 August: I love how you surprise me with exquisite flower bouquets "just because." That's the lavish side of you.

#WILAY 14 August: On the other hand, you can be practical and thrifty. For example, you do the homework before buying a car. You consider all angles: safety, experience with the model, price, fuel economy, reliability, consumer reviews, and trends. I see an electric car in our future.

#WILAY 15 August: You cultivate gratitude.

#WILAY 16 August: I've told you many times, but I love your iPhone recording: "Hi! This is Paul!" I love it so much that sometimes I want the calls to go directly to voicemail so I can hear that sexy voice again.

#WILAY 17 August: You help others solve problems at work and at home.

#WILAY 18 August: I love your sense of humor.

#WILAY 19 August: You like to explore cool, hidden, and unusual places.

#WILAY 20 August: You help me follow my dreams, like becoming an author.

#WILAY 21 August: You're always there, rain or shine.

#WILAY 22 August: You have a heart of gold: a kind and generous disposition.

#WILAY 23 August: Your eyes smile when you laugh.

#WILAY 24 August: Your energy is positive and bright.

#WILAY 25 August: You give warmhearted embraces.

#WILAY 26 August: You are truthful and vulnerable with me.

#WILAY 27 August: You care about my opinion and include me in all important decisions.

#WILAY 28 August: You nourish your relationships with family and friends.

#WILAY 29 August: You chose me and continue to choose me.

#WILAY 30 August: You are reliable. Your motto is "to be early is to be on time, to be on time is to be late."

#WILAY 31 August: As a gentle summer breeze blows across our bed, you hold me close while I fall asleep.

Chapter Nine

September

#WILAY 01 September: As summer collapses into autumn, you sit quietly beside me and watch leaves turn vibrant shades of scarlet, saffron, and auburn before drifting into the crisp air. We're grounded and settled as we relish God's grand finale of the year.

#WILAY 02 September: You are my comfort zone. Wherever you are, I am home.

#WILAY 03 September: I love how we can talk all night and never run out of things to say.

#WILAY 04 September: You can brighten my mood just by walking into a room.

#WILAY 05 September: You have taught me that our first and last love is self-love, and if you can't love and respect yourself, then no one else will be able to either.

#WILAY 06 September: You inspire me daily. Your love reminds me that nothing is impossible.

#WILAY 07 September: I love how you look; your qualities and characteristics, your life story, your quirks, and everything that makes you unique.

#WILAY 08 September: You always voice your opinion confidently when you could more easily nod along and take the road of least resistance to avoid conflict.

#WILAY 09 September: You make me feel special when you describe our time together as "blissful." And you repeat, "We are together. We are together. We are together."

#WILAY 10 September: You have successfully worked through conflicts and messy situations in the relationships that matter to you.

#WILAY 11 September: You consistently do your very best for others without expecting anything in return.

#WILAY 12 September: Even when it wasn't easy to relate to another's situation, you put in the effort to understand them.

#WILAY 13 September: Being a father figure was the most magnificent thing you ever did. The bond that links you to your children is not one of blood but everlasting love, joy, and respect.

#WILAY 14 September: You never tire of hearing my same anecdotes over and over.

#WILAY 15 September: You enjoy reruns of shows you watched as a child. I find that adorable.

#WILAY 16 September: There have been times when some tasks were challenging, but you did them anyway.

#WILAY 17 September: There are some things you do so well that others remember you for them, like entertaining friends with magic shows and tricks.

#WILAY 18 September: I love your strength.

#WILAY 19 September: Our adventures leave a lasting impression. For instance, whenever we see blazing sunlight reflected onto a glass pane at dusk, we recall a dolphin cruise on the North Carolina sound. The captain's mate told tales and spoke of "fire in the windows" in his seaman's vernacular.

#WILAY 20 September: You want me to be happy.

#WILAY 21 September: You always remember special dates like birthdays and anniversaries.

#WILAY 22 September: You are attentive to my emotional needs.

#WILAY 23 September: You are my confidant. I know I can talk with you about anything.

#WILAY 24 September: You see me with your heart rather than with your eyes.

#WILAY 25 September: I love your sweet disposition.

#WILAY 26 September: You never judge me by my past. Instead, you are sensitive to the culmination of all my experiences, both good and bad, and with all things considered, you accept me just the way I am.

#WILAY 27 September: You never make demands, only requests or suggestions.

#WILAY 28 September: I love your spontaneity and how you enjoy trying new and exciting things.

#WILAY 29 September: I love how you understand my two favorite love languages are physical touch and words of affirmation.

#WILAY 30 September: You always take the time to talk to me. You understand that sometimes all I need is for you to listen.

Chapter Ten

October

#WILAY 01 October: You realize the most sensitive part of my body is not my neckline, breasts, inner thighs, or behind my ears. No, it's my mind.

#WILAY 02 October: You can strike up interesting conversations with anyone. I enjoy listening as you share likes, dislikes, and opinions on topics such as blogs, entertainment, and current events.

#WILAY 03 October: In couple's sessions, we learned to pivot from blame-based thinking to a solution-based mindset. We work toward positive change, and that keeps our relationship growing.

#WILAY 04 October: I love knowing that I'm not your "main squeeze." I'm the only one.

#WILAY 05 October: You are secure enough in yourself and our relationship to step back and let me do my own thing, like writing. You're my biggest fan!

#WILAY 06 October: You appreciate the importance of time apart to focus on ourselves. Thanks for giving me time and space for writing, yoga, hair appointments, spa treatments, and bonding with girlfriends.

#WILAY 07 October: You introduced me to kayaking in the marsh, lovemaking in the sand, and wild horses trotting in the surf of Carolina beaches. All good things are wild and free.

#WILAY 08 October: You know exactly what it takes to make me happy.

#WILAY 09 October: You surprise me with my favorite flowers for the finest reason of all—no reason.

#WILAY 10 October: You use the words "us" and "we" more than "me" and "I" when you talk about the future. I feel secure knowing you see me as a part of your future.

#WILAY 11 October: You set high standards for yourself.

#WILAY 12 October: I love when you send romantic text messages in the middle of the day, because then I know you're thinking about me.

#WILAY 13 October: You always select charming cards that I keep by my bedside and on my desk year-round.

#WILAY 14 October: You remind me to accept what is, let go of what was, and have confidence in what will be.

#WILAY 15 October: We work companionably out of habit and practice.

#WILAY 16 October: Your lovemaking is exciting, seductive, desirable, alluring, inviting, sensual, sultry, slinky, provocative, tempting, and tantalizing . . . which is all so sexy!

#WILAY 17 October: You are tolerant when I ask questions and seek clarification. Your responses most often prevent a misunderstanding or argument.

#WILAY 18 October: I'm addicted to your scent. It has a magnificent way of transporting me back through time and space to some of the happiest moments of my life.

#WILAY 19 October: I love how your body is attracted to mine. It feels like a magnetic pull. It may be a cliché, but my body is pulled to yours like a magnet is to steel.

#WILAY 20 October: I love how you always make me feel beautiful just the way I am.

#WILAY 21 October: You encourage me to be the absolute best I can be.

#WILAY 22 October: Nothing soothes my soul like walking on the shores of the Outer Banks holding your hand. It's one of life's most supreme pleasures.

#WILAY 23 October: I love your humorous synonyms for body parts. Sometimes I think you make them up as you go along.

#WILAY 24 October: You know when and where to watch the sunlit International Space Station as it orbits overhead and becomes visible in our night sky. That's something cool I love about you.

#WILAY 25 October: I hunger for your touch—how you sensuously run your hand down my arm and ask, "How does that feel?" Next, you move to my hand and ask, "And how about this?" And then further down to my fingers and the delicate pads of my fingertips and ask, "And this?"

#WILAY 26 October: You never make me feel like I am taken for granted.

#WILAY 27 October: I love how you surprise me (every once in a while) by taking on one of my chores.

#WILAY 28 October: You are willing to admit your mistakes and say, "I'm sorry," when appropriate.

#WILAY 29 October: You make me feel deserving of all the love and attention you have to offer.

#WILAY 30 October: You know that experiences are far more valuable than money will ever be.

#WILAY 31 October: I love how you enchant children with magic tricks on Halloween and place me under your love spell.

Chapter Eleven

November

#WILAY 01 November: You kiss in such a way that I can't wait to kiss you again.

#WILAY 02 November: I appreciate how you open up to me and share the good and the bad. It's very telling: You trust me enough to be vulnerable.

#WILAY 03 November: You never criticize or disregard my feelings.

#WILAY 04 November: You have an uncanny ability to bypass my words, "I'm okay" and feel the authentic vibes that convey, "I'm not okay."

#WILAY 05 November: You make my life more meaningful and fulfilling simply by being in it.

#WILAY 06 November: You take me into unchartered territory I never could have imagined.

#WILAY 07 November: No matter how torrential the storm, I can always count on you to protect me from the rain.

#WILAY 08 November: You always guard my honor, whether I'm there to defend myself or not.

#WILAY 09 November: A simple compliment from you can brighten my whole day. I love your attention to the little things, like a new hairstyle or nail color. You appreciate that I take the time to care for myself.

#WILAY 10 November: Your text messages always put a smile on my face.

#WILAY 11 November: I'm proud of your service to our country.

#WILAY 12 November: You don't "find" time for me; you make time. I love how you make our time together a priority.

#WILAY 13 November: Call it old-fashioned, but I love the way we hold hands.

#WILAY 14 November: You never let me fall asleep without knowing that I am truly loved.

#WILAY 15 November: You make love not only to my body but to my mind.

#WILAY 16 November: I rarely leave anything to chance. I'm a careful planner and list maker, but you are the best thing I "never" planned. That is serendipity.

#WILAY 17 November: You are my favorite. My favorite eyes to gaze into. My favorite name to pop up on my phone. My favorite companion. My favorite everything.

#WILAY 18 November: You are a fun accomplice in harmless but sneaky adventures that we shall not disclose in print.

#WILAY 19 November: I am comforted when you run your fingers through my tangled hair and gently stroke my scalp as I rest my weary head upon your chest.

#WILAY 20 November: You are not afraid to explore my fantasies, to turn them into reality (well, most of them anyway). ☺

#WILAY 21 November: You set my mind and body free to be anything and everything without ever being judged.

#WILAY 22 November: You take me to places I've never been, show me things I've never seen, and make me feel like I've never felt.

#WILAY 23 November: All you have to do to capture my attention is to walk into the room. When you move in my direction, it's as though my body has a will all its own and knows what it wants.

#WILAY 24 November: You don't box Thanksgiving into a day on the calendar. You make it a habit to thank people every day. You express your gratitude sincerely and without the expectation of anything in return.

#WILAY 25 November: I love how you sneak behind and slowly guide me toward your body. I melt into your embrace.

#WILAY 26 November: You made me believe in love all over again.

#WILAY 27 November: God made your body to fit mine perfectly.

#WILAY 28 November: I love how you collect memorabilia for a time capsule to preserve our legacy. I pray someone as extraordinary as you will discover the treasures.

#WILAY 29 November: You find humor where others see none. During a tour of the North Carolina Aquarium, you filled an exhibit hall with chuckles and applause from the crowd when you noticed a diver in full gear performing tank maintenance. You bellowed, "Look, everybody! It's a human. I think it's a female!"

#WILAY 30 November: You are like a Boy Scout troop leader. You always leave a space a little bit better than you found it.

Chapter Twelve

December

#WILAY 01 December: Many souls have breathed easier because you have lived.

#WILAY 02 December: I love how a tuxedo accentuates your distinguished, dark, and handsome features. I feel like a princess when I dress up and walk arm in arm beside you.

#WILAY 03 December: You make sacrifices so that I will not have to sacrifice.

#WILAY 04 December: You made me believe there's a way for people like us to end up okay—a believer in happy endings and second chances. Maybe I am so broken I need second chances ad infinitum.

#WILAY 05 December: I get a kick out of watching you flamboyantly demonstrate the operation of contraptions, like the new deluxe wheel barrel and other gadgets. You make an entertaining show that is worth posting for laughs and giggles.

#WILAY 06 December: The six talents of yours I most admire are:

> #1 kissing
> #2 playing music
> #3 managing finances
> #4 organizing
> #5 narrating humorous anecdotes
> #6 kissing some more

#WILAY 07 December: You never let a day go by without a kiss, a hug, and a gentle embrace.

#WILAY 08 December: You value quality of friendships over the quantity.

#WILAY 09 December: I adore your soft, gentle side.

#WILAY 10 December: I'm impressed by how much you know about so many different things.

#WILAY 11 December: I love how we talk about erotic fantasies and sometimes turn them into reality. Tell me one tonight.

#WILAY 12 December: I love our daily ritual of texting at the noon hour.

#WILAY 13 December: I love how you surprise me with date nights to cultural events such as a recreation of Edgar Allen Poe's public readings under the stars. An acrostic poem written by Poe is entitled simply *An Acrostic*. Here's a shorter verse written by me:

> **P**aul
>
> **A**ntoinette
>
> **U**nconditional
>
> **L**ove

#WILAY 14 December: Sometimes you make time stop and fly simultaneously, just like you make my heart stop and race.

#WILAY 15 December: You always know where to find the silver lining.

#WILAY 16 December: The way you cherish your loved ones is touching. I'm glad to be one of them.

#WILAY 17 December: You know how to get the most out of life—to live, love, and laugh.

#WILAY 18 December: You try to cure me of exceeding my limits. Enjoying things in moderation is so much better!

#WILAY 19 December: I love the shoulder I've always leaned on as we've walked hand in hand through some of life's momentous events.

#WILAY 20 December: You are my BFF. Lack of love does not end marriages and relationships, but a lack of friendship does. I am so lucky to be your best friend, too.

#WILAY 21 December: You don't care that I have slightly protuberant front teeth, a mouth that could have used orthodontia. All I want for Christmas are two new front teeth. 🐰

#WILAY 22 December: I never tire of listening to stories about your childhood and growing up in New England. Here's one I call Jazz Man: Once upon a time, a handsome boy exchanged his snare drum for a slide trombone because his elementary music teacher needed someone to play trombone in the band. He's been playing trombone ever since, even in the U.S. Army band. The rest is history. 🎺

#WILAY 23 December: You can distinguish constellations in the bejeweled night sky like Venus, our bright planetary neighbor.

#WILAY 24 December: I love how you value experiences over physical gifts. A favorite is visiting picturesque Christmas Town destinations, places so magical it's like stepping into a Hallmark movie scene. Then again, there's no place like home for the holidays, and nothing is better than snuggling with a mug of hot chocolate and bingeing on holiday films like *A Christmas Carol*.

#WILAY 25 December: I love how you thoughtfully find meaning-ful gifts that reflect a personal connection we shared or capture the essence of a significant time in our lives. You know what matters to me. You've given me so much, and the greatest gift of all is your love.

#WILAY 26 December: There was a time you could have easily taken advantage of me, but you chose to remain the respectful gentleman you are.

#WILAY 27 December: I love your quirky analogies.

#WILAY 28 December: Being around you makes everything better.

#WILAY 29 December: Actions speak louder than words, and your actions tell an incredible story.

#WILAY 30 December: Because of you, I will leave plenty of white space on my new year's calendar. During the most mundane times, eureka moments happen, and I gain fresh perspectives. White space allows time for my thoughts to drift to you.

#WILAY 31 December: I could go on and on and on. There are so many things that I could thank you for. But most importantly, thank you for showing me what it means to truly love and to be loved in return. I will spend every day of the coming year imagining how I might do a little better living up to the greatest gift I've been given.

Final Entry

#WILAY 01 January: For all of these reasons, I love you more than yesteryear. You always leave me wanting more.

This story of why I love you has no end.

You will be in a sequel in my next lifetime.

Love Notes

Image by Gordon Johnson from Pixabay

Let's give 'em something to text about.

Here are a few tips for writing your messages.

Think of specific things you love about him.

Think about his unique talents and how those things have improved your life and relationship.

Have a good mix of funny, sexy, and serious reasons why you love him.

Save favorite quotes that remind you of your love for him.

About the Author

Antoinette "Stormy" Weathers is a lifetime resident of Hampton, Virginia. As a retired nurse, she turned to a second career in writing that is equally rewarding. She enjoys gardening, yoga, book clubs, and spending time with her white German Shepherd, Winter Weathers. Winter has become a writing companion, always curled up at her feet.

Antoinette has always been motivated to help others. *In Leadership in Retrospect: From the Stretcher-Side to the Boardroom*, she presents a professional approach to survival in healthcare. Today, the author proposes a simple, two-minute phenomenon to enhance your personal life. #WILAY is a private collection of messages for texting an affirmation, encouragement, or other positive comment to make the person on the receiving end more satisfied with your relationship. Replicate the samples with personal touches. #WILAY is not a book destined for a library shelf, but one the author hopes will become a companion and well-thumbed source of inspiration.

Acknowledgments

Brandi Reichenbach
Professional Librarian

Feedback is a gift. Despite writing experience, authors are often blind to flaws and blunders because we are so close to our work. For this reason, I am indebted to Brandi Reichenbach, who delivered discernment and a thoughtful critique from a reader's perspective.

Michael Roberts
Author of *Savannah Girl Series*

Michael Roberts scrutinized this manuscript with an eye trained for the craft of writing. He provided candid and constructive criticism.

I appreciate Michael's refining touches to #WILAY.

CPSIA information can be obtained
at www.ICGtesting.com
Printed in the USA
JSHW072226201222
35258JS00007B/76